STAGECOACH MERSEYSIDE

SIMON ACKERS

AMBERLEY

First published 2024

Amberley Publishing
The Hill, Stroud
Gloucestershire, GL5 4EP

www.amberley-books.com

Copyright © Simon Ackers, 2024

The right of Simon Ackers to be identified as
the Author of this work has been asserted in
accordance with the Copyrights, Designs and
Patents Act 1988.

ISBN 978 1 3981 2270 3 (print)
ISBN 978 1 3981 2271 0 (ebook)

British Library Cataloguing in Publication Data.
A catalogue record for this book is available from
the British Library.

Origination by Amberley Publishing.
Printed in the UK.

Introduction

The thing that I have always liked about Amberley publications is that they can be one of two things at the relevant time: either a book to pick up at random moments and open at an equally random page, or a book that tells a story of a particular period of time relating to a specific topic that you're interested in. So where to begin with the story of Stagecoach Merseyside?

Stagecoach was founded in 1980 by brother and sister Brian Souter and Ann Gloag, running coaches between Scotland and London. With deregulation, in 1986 Magic Bus was launched in Glasgow and in 1987 Stagecoach invested in several National Bus Company businesses. What followed was continuous growth and expansion, not just in Britian and buses but globally and across transport modes. However, Stagecoach buses (apart from second-hand examples) did not appear on the streets of Merseyside until 2005 when they acquired Gillmoss Garage.

Gillmoss Garage, located on the East Lancashire Road in the north-east corner of Liverpool, was opened in 1962 by Liverpool Corporation Passenger Transport before passing to the Merseyside Passenger Transport Executive (MPTE) on its formation in 1969. At deregulation it passed to Merseybus/MTL and was the operating base for routes to the north and east of Liverpool and Kirkby. When Arriva purchased MTL in 2000 the garage had an allocation of 168 buses made up of ex-London Leyland Titans, Volvo Olympians, Volvo B10Bs, Volvo B6s, and low-floor Scania L113s and Dennis Darts.

With Arriva already having a presence on Merseyside, they were instructed to sell a proportion of the business by the Competition Commission. This meant not just some buses but an operating base too, and Gillmoss was chosen, but not as it was in 2000. A number of the more profitable routes were transferred to other garages along with some of the more modern vehicles, essentially leaving the Kirkby network of services. In July 2001 the newly formed Glenvale Transport acquired Gillmoss.

Glenvale would enjoy a period of expansion, assisted by the ruling that Arriva could not compete on the network that had just been sold, but there was no restriction the other way, which Glenvale made the most of and registered on many of the most profitable services across the city. To do this required more vehicles, which came through the acquisition of local rival CMT Buses and from the purchase of second-hand vehicles, many of which were ex-Stagecoach. In 2004 Arriva were able to start competing against Glenvale, and proceeded to do so, which along with rising debt and a lack of fleet investment, led to them being put up for sale.

Enter Stagecoach. Although relatively close to Stagecoach Manchester and Stagecoach North West, Stagecoach Merseyside would be established as its own entity in July 2006 following an £11.2 million deal (£3.4 million plus the absorption of £7.8 million of debt). The Glenvale fleet received Stagecoach logos and fleet numbers, and very quickly mid-life Volvo B10Ms and Olympians were drafted in from across the country to help reduce the age profile of the fleet. The B10Bs and Darts of CMT would be repainted, but most of the acquired vehicles would stay for little more than a year. £5.6 million was invested in new buses within a month, with seventy-five Alexander Dennis Darts ordered. Of these, thirty were diverted from an existing order and began to arrive as early as the September. Route and operational rationalisation was undertaken, and the service numbers can be seen disappearing throughout the first part of this book, as much of the competition with Arriva was gradually removed. Very quickly the beachball of Stagecoach was well established.

In 2011 there was a restructuring of Stagecoach's UK bus operations, with Stagecoach North West split in half. The Preston and Chorley operations were merged with Merseyside to become Stagecoach Merseyside & South Lancashire.

The Merseyside presence would increase in 2013 when Stagecoach purchased the Rock Ferry (Birkenhead) and Chester operations of First for £4.5 million. Rock Ferry came with a history not of MTL and MPTE, but of Crosville. What it did have in common with Gillmoss was the need for fleet investment, and a batch of Enviro300s destined for Liverpool were instead hastily diverted to the Wirral.

At the start of 2024 Stagecoach had 176 and sixty-five vehicles allocated to Gillmoss and Rock Ferry respectively. Both garages operate a mixture of commercial and tendered services, with both gaining significant work in the respective Merseytravel services to schools contract rounds. The fleet profile has become quite standardised: double deckers are either Enviro400MMC or Enviro400s and single deckers are Enviro300 or Enviro200s. There are some variations underneath but to the casual observer things look pretty similar. Of course, there are always some exceptions.

What this book will do is start with what the fleet looked like when Stagecoach took over and chart the seventeen-and-a-half-year journey to the end of 2023. Whether you are looking through it sat on the sofa or passing two and a half hours on a peak X2 journey, I hope it evokes some memories and you learn at least one thing you didn't know already.

As ever, this is also my opportunity to record my thanks to my family for putting up with all of the lost hours as I compiled this book, to colleagues for the assistance in contributing and clarifying the gaps and uncertainties, and to those at Amberley for taking me on this publishing journey.

Glenvale had inherited a lot of the MTL ex-London Leyland Titans when they acquired Gillmoss, but A850 SUL had been purchased from Stagecoach Devon in 2001. It lasted less than a year back with its former owner and was withdrawn in February 2006 as Stagecoach moved to modernise the Merseyside fleet. It is seen here in Norris Green not looking in the best of shape.

Ex-London and then MTL Leyland Titan 2703 had been transferred from Green Lane depot to Gillmoss ahead of the Arriva sale, eventually being repainted into 'Glenvale red' and named *Firecracker*. It is pictured here taking layover at Mann Island, when it was withdrawn soon after it had been in service for twenty-three years.

Wright Renown-bodied Volvo B10BLE 21107 and Wright Endurance-bodied Volvo B10B 21013, both new to CMT, take layover at Paradise Street bus station amidst Arriva vehicles. 21013 would go on to operate with local independent operator Peoplesbus.

Stagecoach didn't just reacquire some Leyland Titans when they purchased Glenvale; they also got back over fifty Alexander Dash-bodied Dennis Darts and Volvo B6s. None would be repainted into Stagecoach livery. L441 LWA had come from Stagecoach East Midland in 2004.

The newest buses that were at Gillmoss were five Pointer 2-bodied Dennis Darts that were new to CMT in 2002. 33177 is seen here in Bootle and would stay in the Stagecoach fleet, eventually transferring to Preston depot.

The Alexander PS-bodied Volvo B10M was the quick fix for reducing the age profile of the fleet. 20934 was new to Stagecoach Manchester in 1997 and is seen departing Queen Square bus station, the driver still in Glenvale uniform.

34477 was a Transbus Dart SLF new to Stagecoach North West in 2004 but was one of over sixty vehicles damaged in flooding at Carlisle just a year later. Initially written off, the damage was later assessed to be economically repairable, and the batch of Darts found a new home on Merseyside. The 'T' after the fleet number stood for 'Tide Damage'.

34749 was one of the first new buses to arrive for Stagecoach Merseyside, part of a batch of thirty that came from an existing order of Alexander Dennis Darts. Here it loads at Paradise Street bus station on the service it would soon receive route branding for.

20603 had a short visit to Merseyside, a Northern Counties-bodied Volvo B10M that was new to Stagecoach South and would then move to Stagecoach Manchester. It is on service 217 to Halewood, a route that would be shortened (quite considerably) when Stagecoach came to implement their network/operational reviews at various points in 2006.

32921 arrives at Paradise Street bus station, a Northern Counties-bodied Dennis Dart that was new to CMT in 1995 and had been repainted quite quickly into Stagecoach livery. The building work in the background is the construction of the Liverpool ONE shopping area that would significantly alter the look (for the better) and appeal of a large part of the city centre. These were the final few days before Paradise Street bus station would close in November 2005 and move to the new Liverpool ONE bus station.

Alexander-bodied Leyland Olympians were cascaded from the North East to support the Gillmoss operations. 14076 is pictured in the newly opened Liverpool ONE bus station on service 27, one of the many Arriva routes that Glenvale had registered in competition.

34743 was one of the new Darts. When the bus station moved most of the services transferred too. But unfortunately, passengers didn't make the move: the bus station opened as one of the first parts of the Liverpool ONE construction, so the pedestrian access was not the best and the journey times around the city centre meant passengers would go to other city centre stops. Gradually services would be withdrawn to use on street layover instead, and it would be many years until the footfall in Liverpool ONE bus station increased.

30146 was one of the ex-MTL Plaxton Pointer-bodied Volvo B6s. Here it leaves the layover area of Liverpool ONE bus station to head back to the bus station to enter service.

Another of the Leyland Olympians is at Bootle bus station about to depart on cross-city service 60, another of the routes competing with Arriva that would soon be withdrawn.

Dart 34758 turns from Lime Street into St George's Place, now carrying route branding for services 20/21 but operating on a 12 from Stockbridge Village. This was a former Gillmoss route in the MTL days, which Arriva had transferred to Green Lane before the sale. It was another that Glenvale had tried to compete on.

Dart 34807 makes the same turn from Lime Street into St George's Place as 34758. In terms of dates this photo sits out of place, however it shows in the background the work that was being carried out in the previous photo on the plateaux area outside of Lime Street station.

34809 was part of the second batch of Darts that were delivered, these forty-five being a new order worth £3.9 million. Service 80 was one that CMT had originally operated against MTL and then Arriva, but the location of Gillmoss did not lend itself to marginal south city routes, so it would soon be withdrawn as Stagecoach consolidated their network to help the business grow sustainably.

The 86 and 82 routes were certainly not marginal services, so were not pending a 2006 withdrawal when this shot was taken of one of the B10Ms leading a Dart to their busy pick-up points.

I didn't think it was going to be possible to have a picture of an 18 in this book, but then in the collection I found one. Yet another service that Glenvale had tried to compete against Arriva on, B10M 20306 heads through Liverpool city centre. This example was a former Scottish one rather than from Manchester.

Dart 34751 loads in Queen Square bus station in 2006. If you want to chart the increasing cost of travel, a day ticket then cost £2.40.

21073 was a Wright Liberator-bodied Volvo B10L new to CMT in 1998. Here it exits Skelhorne Street whilst on diversion during a closure of Hanover Street.

34217 was a MPD (Mini Pointer Dart) that came from London, and though pictured here unbranded it would soon gain branding for the 197/198 Kirkby local services, and also be preserved in model form.

33179 was one of the CMT Transbus Darts, repainted into Stagecoach livery and traveling along Dale Street in Liverpool city centre.

33145, an East Lancs Spryte-bodied Dennis Dart, was one of eight that Glenvale had acquired from local operator Express Travel in 2003. It is arriving at Bootle bus station on Merseytravel contract service 135.

Other than the Titans and B6s, which did not last long, the only other ex-MTL vehicles that Stagecoach had were some Marshall Capital-bodied Dennis Darts. 33172 was previously 7610 and would soon be transferred to Preston.

With the acquisition of Glenvale came service 284 between Liverpool and Southport, where it met the existing Stagecoach Preston to Southport service. In the summer of 2006, the X2 was introduced running all the way from Preston to Liverpool, originally operated with a coach allocation. 52414 is pictured in Preston bus station.

Wright Renown-bodied Volvo B10BLE 21118 was given a special Liverpool-themed livery in 2006 as part of the Liverpool Biennial celebrations, a contemporary visual arts festival that took place across the city. 21118 reappears later in the book in another special livery.

The construction cranes at Liverpool ONE tower over the city centre skyline as two Kirkby-bound buses wait to exit Queen Square bus station in late 2006.

In 2007 Stagecoach partnered with Liverpool Football Club to wrap Dart 34815 in a special livery celebrating the latter's success in European football. Dart 34770 was given an Everton Football Club wrap, but I'm unsure what that was celebrating.

34770 was, quite appropriately given its registration plate, the Everton Football Club bus. (Photo by Graham Judge)

Preston's Alexander RL-bodied Volvo Olympian 16328 is seen at Bootle Strand filling in on the X2.

21111 was part of a batch of ten Wright Renown-bodied Volvo B10BLEs that CMT purchased at the end of 1998.

Always a grand backdrop, St George's Hall sits behind B10M 20319 as it heads out to Netherley.

Taking layover on Castle Street is ex-CMT Dart 33178.

21073 makes a second appearance, on this occasion from early 2008 while carrying an all-over advert for B&Q. The uncovered panel appears too close to the paint roller to be accidental.

Registration S22 ABC was originally on an Optare Solo that was owned by ABC Travel, who sold to CMT, etc. That bus moved to Preston and the registration plate was transferred to Dart 34817. A day ticket now costs £2.80.

A trio of the 2005 Darts are seen in a busy Queen Square bus station.

By 2008 the coaches on the X2 had been replaced by route branded Northern Counties-bodied Volvo Olympians that had come from London and been converted to single-door operation. 16447 loads ahead of the 39-mile trip to Preston.

Gillmoss also received some ex-London Volvo Olympians, albeit a year later than the Preston ones. However, these were originally with Go-Ahead London Central, and came to the Stagecoach fleet through the acquisition of Yorkshire Traction. 16870 is travelling along Hanover Street, soon to arrive at Liverpool ONE bus station.

In 2009 the X2 had another change of vehicles, with Preston depot receiving new low-floor Enviro400-bodied Scania N230UDs. 15468 would end up at Birkenhead depot when the next new vehicles came for the service.

In late 2009 and early 2010 the next new buses began to arrive at Gillmoss. Forty-five Alexander Dennis Enviro300-bodied MAN 18.240s were delivered and represented an increase in capacity on the busier routes. 24153 was one that received branding for services 20/21, with the Darts cascaded to a different allocation.

24171 is pictured taking layover in Liverpool city centre.

24125 was branded for service 14, and is pictured on Lime Street arriving into Liverpool city centre.

24175 was branded for the 10A and is pictured arriving into St Helens town centre.

The construction cranes have gone from the skyline above and behind these two Dennis Darts, ex-Express Travel East Lancs Spryte-bodied 33149 and Alexander Dennis-bodied 34764.

34745 travels through Liverpool city centre.

To alleviate overcrowding in Queen Square bus station on match days and ensure adequate capacity for football fans, as well as general passengers on services 17 and 19, Stagecoach introduced the 917 and 919 operating direct to Anfield and Goodison respectively. One of the ex-Yorkshire Traction Olympians loads on St John's Lane.

A pair of ex-CMT Wright Liberator-bodied Volvo B10Ls are pictured at the front of their respective lines within Gillmoss depot. Note the different appearance to the front of the two buses.

There had been just the one Magic Bus route in Liverpool, and that was a shorter version of service 14 operated by a batch of B10Ms. 20208 heads the Magic Bus line in Gillmoss, all of them being in much need of a wash.

A Magic Bus visitor from Manchester was 20876, a Northern Counties Paladin-bodied Volvo B10M.

Dart 34810 leaves a snowy Croxteth Park on Merseytravel contracted service 216.

Enviro300-bodied MAN 18.240 24139 turns into Queen Square bus station to commence a 10B journey.

Ex-CMT Wright Renown-bodied Volvo B10BLE 21113 arrives at Queen Square bus station in January 2011, with the price of a day ticket now at £3.10.

In the final days of Magic Bus operation in January 2011, 20210 passes in front of Lime Street station.

Wright Renown-bodied Volvo B10B 21112 leaves Mann Island.

More new Enviro300-bodied buses arrived at Gillmoss in 2011, but this time integral Alexander Dennis versions rather than MANs. 27710 is shiny and new on the 10A.

The 86H was a trial service linking Liverpool South Parkway with Liverpool Hope University, and the vehicle allocation was generally Optare Solos, but not conventional versions. 47709 was part of a BioFuel trial in partnership with Merseytravel. The buses originally operated with Arriva as part of the CATCH (Clean Accessible Transport for Community Health) hybrid-electric trial.

Wright Renown-bodied Volvo B10BLE 21111 turns in front of Lime Street station.

Enviro300 24135 arrives on the 10C, the third variant of the 10 that Stagecoach operated until the introduction of the Quality Partnership on the corridor.

Volvo Olympian 16442 turns in Liverpool ONE bus station, not long before it would transfer to Cumbria.

17201 was an Alexander ALX400-bodied Dennis Trident new to Stagecoach East London in 2000, pictured here on Walton Hall Avenue when newly arrived at Gillmoss. It was originally registered as V201 MEV but given cherished plate VRR 447 that originally belonged to a VanHool coach. The plate would be transferred to a Chester sightseeing bus in 2015.

17283 was another ex-London Dennis Trident given a cherished registration plate. It is parked here in the layover area of Liverpool ONE bus station, and when it left Gilmoss it transferred to Manchester to join the Magic Bus fleet.

TSU 641 was a former coach registration given to 17325. It appears again in the book on a different vehicle – will you spot it?

VKB 708 was a cherished registration plate that was given to Dart 34820. Originally on a Liverpool Corporation Leyland PD2, it had previously been carried by a MerseyCoach and Heysham Travel Sightseers coach. It too reappears later in this book.

Enviro300 24131 manoeuvres around the double roundabout at Broadway, Norris Green, having passed beneath the former loop line railway bridge that now forms an 11-mile traffic-free cycle route between Halewood and Aintree.

Some of the 2011 Enviro300 deliveries received branding for the 10A, 27719 being one of them.

More integral Enviro300s came throughout 2012. 27775 is waiting on James Street to turn onto The Strand to head to Liverpool ONE bus station.

27780 was new to Gillmoss in March 2012 but a couple of years later would transfer across the River Mersey and down to Chester to be route branded for the new X8 service, before later moving down south.

33029 was a Plaxton Pointer-bodied Dennis Dart that came to Merseyside from Stagecoach South, but before that it had started life in Hong Kong, hence the air-conditioning pod on the roof. I remember these having the comfiest seats!

In 2013 the Stagecoach presence on Merseyside grew with the purchase of First's Rock Ferry (Wirral) and Chester depots gaining an additional 100 vehicles. Similarly to the acquisition of Glenvale, the buses received Stagecoach logos and fleet numbers. YJ04 FZF was a Wright Eclipse Gemini-bodied Volvo B7 that became 16965, and while it didn't stay at Rock Ferry long it did remain with Stagecoach, transferring up to Fife and then ending up as an open-topper in Cleethorpes.

An order of integral Alexander Dennis 10.7-metre Enviro200s was diverted to upgrade some of the ex-First fleet. 36819 is departing Liverpool city centre for Chester soon after the takeover.

Services 41/42 on the Wirral received new buses quickly. 36815 passes Rock Ferry station.

The ex-CMT Darts were still at Gillmoss in 2013 but now had standard destination blinds fitted. 33177 is departing Liverpool ONE bus station, the Albert Dock behind it.

The layover point for the 20/21 varied depending on the driver. Some would take it at the terminus on Water Street and others at the start point on James Street. 24162 sits in a flurry of snow on the latter.

The replacements for the Gemini-bodied Volvo B7s at Rock Ferry for the Quality Partnership services 471/472 were Enviro400-bodied Tridents that had been new to Stagecoach Manchester. 19018 is departing Cook Street in Liverpool city centre.

19054 was another Enviro400 that arrived from Manchester, seen here approaching the alighting stop at Whitechapel in Liverpool city centre.

24157 provides a view of St George's Hall from a different angle as it waits to turn onto London Road.

The new buses at Rock Ferry replaced some aging Scanias. Enviro200 36817 departs Birkenhead bus station to the Woodchurch estate.

In 2013 as the Stagecoach Merseyside fleet moved to being 100 per cent low-floor ahead of the scheduled 1 January 2017 deadline (2016 for single deckers) there was another influx of Enviro300s for Gillmoss. 27897 is pictured when new in Liverpool ONE bus station, and would go on to have spells at Preston, on loan at Fife, and then Rock Ferry.

27899 is on Elliot Street. It too would go with 27897 to operate out of Preston, on loan at Fife, before moving to Rock Ferry.

25233 was an Optare Versa, new at Preston in 2008 and branded for service 84 between Fleetwood and Blackpool. In 2014 it had a short stay at Gillmoss.

Before the Enviro400MMC in Stagecoach colours became a common sight on Merseyside, first came stop/start technology demonstrator 80027 in May 2015 and operated on services out of Gillmoss.

In August 2015 80027 was at Rock Ferry and is pictured at Cook Street on cross-river duties. Can you spot the differences from when it was at Gillmoss? When its demonstrating days were over it would become 10430 with Stagecoach Manchester.

Some of the 2012 Enviro300s moved from Gillmoss to Chester depot and were branded for the new X8 service, a more express bus link between Liverpool and Chester. 27777 loads in Sir Thomas Street, Liverpool city centre.

In 2015 Stagecoach's Merseyside competitor, Arriva, began to introduce a lot of double-deck vehicles across the network, giving additional capacity on services and with it improving the passenger experience. In 2016 Stagecoach started to do the same, with the Enviro400MMC becoming a regular delivery in the same way that the Enviro300s had been. At the beginning of 2024 there would be eighty-four between Gillmoss and Rock Ferry.

In November 2017, outside the offices of the Liverpool City Region Combined Authority, Stagecoach launched their new high-spec arrivals. Seven integral Alexander Dennis Enviro400MMC vehicles had been ordered to Stagecoach Gold standard, and eleven Enviro400MMC-bodied Scania N250UDs for the X2.

New to Preston Bus, a batch of East Lancs Esteem-bodied Scania N94UBs spent some time at Gilllmoss, mainly on services to schools but occasionally finding their way into general service. 28513 is seen here in the depot in 2017 not long before it was sold to Maghull Coaches.

Part of the 2017 delivery of Enviro400MMCs was 10843, parked in Gillmoss before being driven by the author.

Here an Enviro300 and an Optare Solo receive some attention on the Gillmoss engineering pits.

One of the withdrawn ex-First Wright Solar-bodied Scania L94UBs sits in Gillmoss alongside withdrawn Trident 18154.

The 14 has always been a flagship service for Gillmoss due to how busy it is and the location in proximity to the depot. 11105, part of the 2018 delivery batch, is pictured at the Croxteth terminus. The depot is just out of shot to the left.

When Avon Buses ceased trading in 2018 Stagecoach won some of the replacement contract work issued by Merseytravel, and Enviro200 36317 transferred from London. It is pictured at Arrowe Park Hospital.

Wright Renown-bodied Volvo B10BLE 21118 was given a repaint into CMT livery, reflecting how it appeared when new in 2000. Here it is on driver training in St Helens.

As part of Liverpool City Council's Connectivity scheme there were extensive roadworks on many key roads in Liverpool city centre between 2019 and 2021. Here the works have reached the junction of Victoria Street and Sir Thomas Street, with the right turn a key movement for buses and almost daily meetings taking place to monitor the traffic management with buses sometimes having just inches of manoeuvrability.

To mark the 100th anniversary of Ribble in 2019 Stagecoach repainted Preston allocated Enviro400-bodied Scania 15566 into the classic Timesaver livery.

10814 is pictured taking part in the first bus test of the Old Haymarket Bus Hub, a new designated layover area for buses terminating at Queen Square bus station.

Enviro400MMC-bodied Scania N250UD 15302 leaves Queen Square bus station for Preston. Due to the length of the journey, it technically breaks at Southport as suggested on the destination blind.

Enviro300 271551 is pictured at Kirkby bus station on the 217A, one of the few four-digit route numbers on Merseyside.

Enviro400MMC 10571 takes layover on Lower Lane outside Aintree Hospital in 2020. The notice in the windscreen is advising people that they must wear face coverings and pay the exact fare only. At this point due to the Covid-19 pandemic change had stopped being given to reduce the cash handling required by drivers, with contactless payments encouraged.

A second Enviro400MMC has arrived to keep 10571 company.

During the capacity restrictions at the height of the pandemic there was a big issue when schools reopened in September 2020. Funding was made available to operate duplicate, closed-door school journeys based on where knowledge and data suggested there were high passenger loadings. Stagecoach operated the S18, two short journeys replicating Arriva's 18 service. 18325, an Alexander ALX400-bodied Trident, new to Stagecoach Manchester, unfortunately broke down one morning.

In 2020 Stagecoach unveiled their new liveries. Local services would receive the white, yellow, green and blue scheme; specialist vehicles would receive a scheme using more green; and longer-distance routes would have a yellow base. On Merseyside all repaints were in the 'Local' scheme, though the specialist livery will make an appearance later. My first photo of the new look was this shot of Enviro300 24136.

A batch of Enviro400-bodied Scania N230UDs transferred up from Stagecoach South, of which 15599 was one, formerly carrying branding for the 700 Coastliner service. Here it travels underneath Rice Lane flyover on the way to Kirkby.

Stagecoach was an official partner of Liverpool's 'China Dream' season in 2018 that featured as part of the Capital of Culture anniversary, celebrating the city's rich links with China. Enviro400-bodied Scania N230UD 15585 was given a special livery to mark the partnership. It still carried the livery when photographed in 2020.

Vehicles tend to pass into the training school towards the end of their fifteen-year operational life. 34743 was training new drivers at the end of 2020, and quite appropriately this bus featured early in this book when it was brand new.

This shot of two 17s laying over at the internal stop at Aintree Hospital shows the two liveries together, and also the 'Face Coverings are Mandatory' on the destination blind. This would alternate with the destination point. This location was a temporary arrangement when works at the main entrance meant buses were unable to circulate. The 17 was given permission to use the ambulance-only access road.

Enviro400MMC 10811 passes through Knowsley Village.

Enviro300-bodied MAN 18.240 24158 takes layover at the Old Haymarket Bus Hub on a very autumnal day.

As part of the 'Better by Bus' campaign, both Arriva and Stagecoach fully wrapped a bus in all-over blue. The Stagecoach vehicle was Enviro400-bodied Scania N230UD 15588, another one of the transfers from Stagecoach South. The registration is another cherished plate from a coach.

The digital destination blind has become more than just something that shows where a bus is going and the service number. The ability to change and not be a static display is utilised for special messages, with probably the most useful one to passengers being that seen here on Enviro400 19570. It highlights to boarding passengers that there may be disruption along their journey so they can get advice from the driver if they will be affected.

Of the seven Gold Enviro400MMC delivered to Rock Ferry, 10888 was the only one never to carry the 471/472 route branding.

Enviro400-bodied Scania N230UD 15610 transferred to Rock Ferry from Stagecoach Oxford giving additional capacity on the 1 to Chester. The interior remains to Stagecoach Gold specification but has since been repainted externally into Local livery.

Merseytravel funds free bus services on Christmas Day to provide a limited service to hospitals. In recent years Stagecoach have won these contracts and in 2021 Optare Solo 47330 was operating the H3. (Photo by Graham Judge)

To commemorate the platinum jubilee of Queen Elizabeth II in 2022 Stagecoach gave Enviro400MMC 10565 a special livery. It is parked here, not in a normal position, at the front of Gillmoss depot.

Kirkby has very much been Stagecoach's dominant area. Enviro400MMC 11112 is about to exit the bus station to head to Tower Hill.

Repainted Enviro400MMC 10572 takes layover outside of the former Conservation Centre in Liverpool city centre.

As part of the Liverpool City Centre Connectivity works, Lime Street outside St George's Hall was reduced to a single lane in either direction. Enviro300 24172 is flanked by some grand architecture, St George's Hall on one side and former Great Western Hotel on the other.

In the summer of 2022 Arriva Merseyside drivers took industrial action over pay, meaning that for twenty-nine consecutive days you only really saw Stagecoach buses in Liverpool city centre, reflected in this morning shot at Old Haymarket.

Queen Square bus station was very quiet for four weeks. 10818 heads to pick up passengers.

In September 2022, with the passing of Queen Elizabeth II, Stagecoach paid their respects with a message on the destination blinds.

2022 saw Enviro400 15743 wear a commemorative livery reflecting Rock Ferry depot's links with Crosville, 'proud to serve the Wirral from Rock Ferry since 1932'.

Enviro400MMC 15305 at Preston depot was given a commemorative livery reflecting the links with Ribble, 'proud to serve Lancashire since 1919'.

In 2022, ahead of the £2 flat fare introduced by the government, the decision had been taken by the Liverpool City Region Combined Authority to use funding received as part of their BSIP (Bus Service Improvement Plan) to support a flat adult fare of £2 to encourage travel by bus. This was promoted in many places, but most eye-catchingly on the destination blinds.

Enviro400MMC 10539 heads outbound along Lime Street.

The location of the Bus Hub on Old Haymarket may have been an ideal dedicated space, but the location meant added circulation time for buses to use it, so if a service arrived in the city centre late because of congestion or other factors it wouldn't have time to be able to call there. Additional layover was therefore provided on Victoria Street, with a trio of repainted Stagecoach vehicles utilising it.

Enviro400MMC 11104 turns in Liverpool ONE bus station to pick up passengers for an outbound trip on the 82.

15749 was another Stagecoach Gold vehicle to transfer to Rock Ferry for the 1 and be repainted, seen here travelling along Victoria Street.

In September 2022 there were some network revisions to reshape the Merseyside network in line with some of the changing post-Covid passenger levels and funding. As part of these, the X3 was sadly withdrawn and replaced with extended journeys on service 17 to serve Knowsley Industrial Park. 10540 travels past the Amazon distribution centre.

A night shot of Enviro400MMC 11113 making use of the Victoria Street layover stands.

All the ones, 11111 is about to turn from Castle Street onto Cook Street. In 2021 nearly all eastern and northern routes had been curtailed to Queen Square bus station, but recognising that there was a peak demand for people to travel further into the city centre some morning journeys extend to Lord Street, where 11111 had just terminated.

Enviro300 24175 sunbathes at the Bus Hub.

Other changes as part of the September 2022 revisions were for the 41/42 to extend from the Woodchurch estate to Arrowe Park Hospital. Enviro300 27895 waits in the layover bay before heading back to Mill Park.

Enviro400MMC 10833 is seen here taking part in a bus test of the 'Lime Street bus link', a bus-only lane across the pedestrianised section of Lime Street to allow buses to access Queen Square bus station. As it waits to exit the linkway, Enviro300 27147 also waits for a green light to proceed to the bus station.

Enviro400MMC 10888 displays a festive message on the destination blind as it loads for Chester.

Enviro400MMC 11107 rests in the Bus Hub on a wet day.

Enviro400MMC 11116 is at Old Haymarket, with the World Museum and Central Library lit up nicely in the background.

27292 replicates the earlier photo of Enviro400MMC 10539 on Lime Street.

10833 makes another appearance, this time posing in the Bus Hub, with Crosville-liveried 15743 visible exiting the Queensway Tunnel.

Enviro400MMC 10819 received the Pride colours to show Stagecoach's LGBTQ+ support. It is pictured here leaving Liverpool ONE bus station.

During the day the layover area at Liverpool ONE bus station is a busy place, with several high-frequency services using it. In the evenings, when Enviro300 24134 can be seen there, it can be much quieter.

15594 is seen here on shuttle bus duties to the Grand National. Each year Stagecoach operates the 922, a direct bus from Liverpool city centre to Aintree Racecourse.

To promote the launch of ITV's new streaming service Enviro400 15586 was given an all-over advert where the logo on the side was illuminated, which this evening shot shows off quite well.

Enviro300 24134 has just terminated in Queen Square bus station and heads to take some layover.

Repainted Enviro400MMC 10837 is pictured in the Bus Hub.

The route of the 1 to Chester from Liverpool is by no means as direct as the train, but it does serve a number of key locations, such as the Countess of Chester Hospital, Cheshire Oaks Designer Outlet, and the most important one for animal lovers: Chester Zoo. 15745 picks up at the stop conveniently located near the zoo entrance.

In May 2023 Eurovision came to Liverpool, with the city chosen to host the event on behalf of Ukraine due to the conflict with Russia. A lot of work went into planning bus services impacted by some of the events, and on 7 May as part of the opening ceremony 10841 was on Park & Ride duties. However, in this shot it has been pulled onto the city centre shuttle to help with the passenger demand to get to London Road where many services were having to terminate.

Enviro400MMC 10814 received a special Eurovision livery that replicated the look of banners, posters, bus stop wraps, and much more. The city and the people well and truly embraced the two-week festival and atmosphere that is Eurovision and all it stands for. 10814 is pictured here waiting to start evening shuttle duties from the fan park at the Pier Head to the Camp & Furnace.

Here is a rear and nearside view of the Eurovision livery.

To mark the coronation of King Charles III Enviro400MMC 10565 was updated to carry this commemorative livery.

Destination blinds on all vehicles were also updated to mark the coronation.

10541 is pictured travelling along Hanover Street, Liverpool city centre.

In 2020 Stagecoach had won the EL1 contract, the shuttle service between Ormskirk rail station and Edge Hill University. Pride-liveried 10819 is pictured at the university in July 2023. (Photo by Graham Judge)

Over the summer of 2023 Stagecoach operated the 'Coastal Breezer' connecting the Mersey Ferry at Seacombe terminal to New Brighton. Alexander ALX400-bodied Dennis Trident 17502 was new to Stagecoach East London in 2001, transferring to Merseyside in 2011. It was converted to open-top for use on sightseeing tours around Chester until being withdrawn in 2021. The cherished plate (that appeared earlier on 17325) helps to hide the vehicle's age!

Twenty Alexander Dennis Enviro400FCEV hydrogen-fuelled vehicles were purchased by Liverpool City Region Combined Authority and then leased to Arriva and to Stagecoach for use on service 10A between Liverpool and St Helens. As well as being zero-emission vehicles, the internal specification is the highest there has been for new buses on Merseyside, with bespoke moquette and coving designs, USB charging and mobile device holders on the seatbacks, audio visual next stop announcements, and much more. The ten for Stagecoach arrived in July 2023 but problems with fuel supply delayed their introduction to service.

In June 2023 Stagecoach announced that they would be acquiring the bus services, contracts, twenty-three vehicles, and twenty-one employees of independent operator Peoplesbus on 9 July 2023. The work consisted of commercial and contracted school services, Merseytravel contracts, and football services. Alexander ALX400-bodied Dennis Trident 18539 was new to Stagecoach East London in 2002 and is pictured here heading the line of ex-Peoplesbus vehicles in Gillmoss depot.

Dual-doored Alexander Dennis Enviro200 36590 was new to Stagecoach East London in 2011 as 36276 and then operated with Arriva London before being acquired by Peoplesbus via Ensignbus in 2023. Having been in an all-white livery it received the 'specialist vehicle' corporate livery with the 'extra green', pictured on Marsh Lane in Bootle. (Photo by Graham Judge)

The location of Gillmoss depot makes it ideal for operating services to schools in the St Helens area, particularly Rainford. Enviro300 27146 is ready to leave to operate a morning 783 journey.

Using their BSIP funding, Lancashire County Council introduced a new Train Link service between Skelmersdale and Kirkby. Stagecoach won the contract, and two Enviro300s were painted into a special livery. 27270 was previously a Stagecoach Gold vehicle at Rock Ferry for the 1 to Chester.

18536, previously registered L90 BUS, is pictured at the Wirral Transport Show in October 2023.

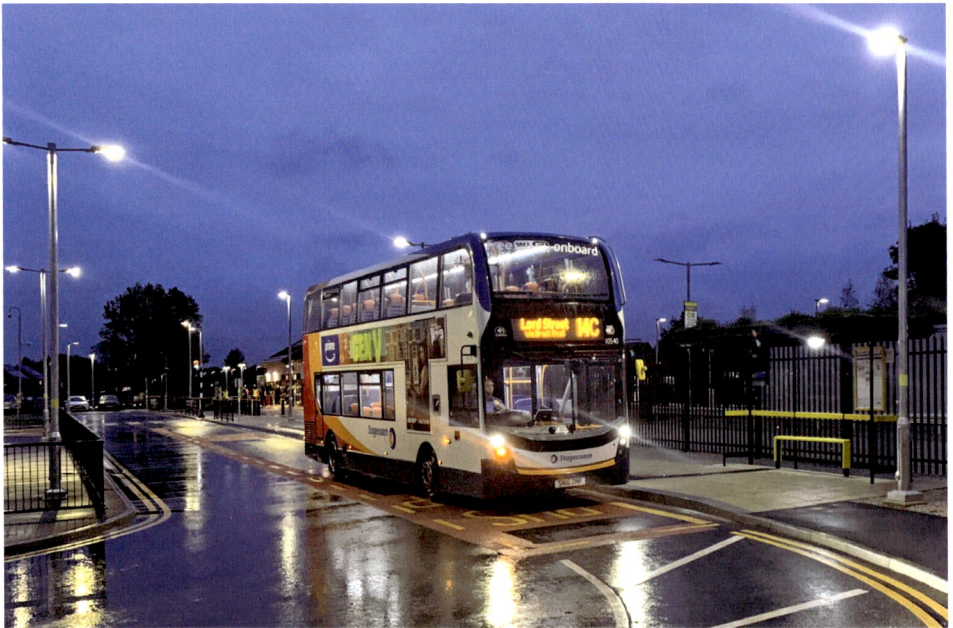

The new Headbolt Lane station in Kirkby opened in 2023. Enviro400MMC 10540, previously seen driving past the Amazon site, was one of the first buses to call there in service on 5 October 2023. (Photo by Tony Killen)

Enviro400MMC 11103 is seen here stopped outside the former Municipal Building on Dale Street in Liverpool city centre. As with many of the significant buildings in the city centre, it is now a hotel.

Stagecoach has an ongoing commitment to support the armed forces, annually offering free travel to serving and ex-military personnel on Armed Forces Day, Remembrance Day, and Remembrance Sunday. They also have an employee-led Veterans Network. Gillmoss-allocated Enviro400MMC 10534 carries the poppy livery supporting the British Legion, and also carries the cherished registration plate from the Liverpool Corporation, PD2.

Preston depot also has a poppy bus in the form of 15301.

Optare Solo 47335, new to Preston depot, is seen here at Kirkby station on its usual allocation, 97 Kirkby local service.

Enviro300 24166 is about to circulate Liverpool ONE bus station to depart on an outbound journey but without yet having changed the destination blind.

Enviro400MMC 11115 passes in front of the Chinese Arch at the top of Liverpool's Chinatown. The arch was imported piece by piece from Shanghai, and standing at 13.5 metres tall is the tallest standing arch in any Chinatown outside of mainland China.

A morning Stagecoach trio at the Bus Hub.

The works carried out on Lime Street certainly made an aesthetic difference to the location, as former Stagecoach Gold-liveried Enviro300 27256 travels inbound.

Three different bus types; three different liveries. Enviro400MMC 11112 arrived at Gillmoss in late 2018 and is flanked by two buses both new in 2009: ex-Peoplesbus Enviro400 19901 was new to First London and then with Metroline, while Enviro 300 24159 was new to Gillmoss for services 20/21.

Enviro300 27153 is pictured taking layover on Dale Street, Liverpool city centre. The journeys on the 17 that extended to Knowsley Industrial Park were given an 'A' suffix to help differentiate which ones extended beyond Aintree Hospital. The area has officially been named 'Knowsley Industrial Park' to enhance the image and reputation, but to many it still is and always will be 'Kirkby Admin'. Full nostalgia would be for the destination blind to show 'Kirkby Admin Gate'.

Although this photograph was taken outside Preston railway station, the bus is heading to Merseyside. The 2, operating from Preston depot with the X2, will, as the destination blind says, end up in Southport. 15230 was new to Preston in Stagecoach Gold livery for the 125 and is the second bus in this book to have been represented in diecast model form.

Repainted Enviro400MMC 10542 is laying over on Victoria Street.

In the summer and early autumn of 2023 thirty-one new Alexander Dennis Enviro400MMC vehicles were delivered, with eight being allocated to Rock Ferry for the 1/X1 and the others going to Preston. 11624 is pictured in front of the Municipal Building in Liverpool city centre.

11679 is seen about to terminate at Whitechapel.

The 157 was a Merseytravel contract previously operated by Peoplesbus. The service links the northern towns and villages of St Helens and into Greater Manchester, with the passenger usage and the nature of some of the roads making it ideal for Mercedes Sprinters. 44019 is pictured on Omskirk Road, Rainford. (Photo by Graham Judge)

The 235 was another Merseytravel contract gained via the Peoplesbus acquisition. Enviro200 36813 is seen on Oriel Road in front of Bootle Town Hall. (Photo by Graham Judge)

Enviro400 19570 is seen here in Kirkby bus station in December 2023, having moved to Gillmoss from Rock Ferry a year earlier. It was previously with Stagecoach South West, and previously seen showing the 'Diversion on Route' destination blind. New for the Exeter Park & Ride, it carried a special livery that it wears in the model that was produced, making it three buses in this book that could be sat in your display cabinet.

Enviro400MMC 10569 demonstrates a full-lock turn into Kirkby bus station.

The Maghull Circulars are a group of Merseytravel contracted routes that particularly link to the rail network to offer onward travel. Stagecoach won this contract in the autumn of 2023, and pictured here is Enviro200 36813 departing for Lydiate.

Enviro400MMC 10822 loads in a brightly lit Liverpool ONE bus station to depart on service 86 to Liverpool South Parkway.

Enviro400-bodied Scania N230UD 15565 was new to Preston depot in 2009 and transferred to Gillmoss in September 2023, seen here about to depart Kirkby bus station.

Due to a number of buses being off the road at Gillmoss in December 2023, vehicles from Preston and Birkenhead depots were brought in for temporary cover. Here the 217 gets the Stagecoach Gold treatment with Preston's Enviro400-bodied Scania N230UD 15249 travelling through Kirkby.

15745, seen earlier at Chester Zoo, was another loanee to Gillmoss but from Rock Ferry, and has just passed Kirkby station as it heads to the bus station and then on to Northwood.

Enviro300 24130 takes layover on a quiet night in Liverpool city centre.